SAN FRANCISCO
49ERS

by Brian Lester

Published by ABDO Publishing Company, 8000 West 78th Street, Edina, Minnesota 55439. Copyright © 2011 by Abdo Consulting Group, Inc. International copyrights reserved in all countries. No part of this book may be reproduced in any form without written permission from the publisher. SportsZone™ is a trademark and logo of ABDO Publishing Company.

Printed in the United States of America,
North Mankato, Minnesota
062010
092010

Editor: Chrös McDougall
Copy Editor: Nicholas Cafarelli
Interior Design and Production: Christa Schneider
Cover Design: Christa Schneider

Photo Credits: Greg Trott/AP Images, cover, 40, 44; AP Images, 1, 4, 10, 15, 16, 19, 20, 22, 27, 31, 42 (top), 42 (middle), 42 (bottom); Lennox McLendon/ AP Images, 7; Rusty Kennedy/AP Images, 8; Harry Harris/AP Images, 13; William Smith/AP Images, 25; Phil Huber/AP Images, 28, 43 (top); Jon Gapps III/AP Images, 33, 43 (middle); NFL Photos/AP Images, 34, 37; Susan Ragan/ AP Images, 35; Lynne Sladky/AP Images, 38; Bob Galbraith/AP Images, 43 (bottom); Julia Robertson/AP Images, 47

Library of Congress Cataloging-in-Publication Data

Lester, Brian, 1975-
  San Francisco 49ers / Brian Lester.
    p. cm. — (Inside the NFL)
  Includes index.
  ISBN 978-1-61714-027-3
  1. San Francisco 49ers (Football team)—History—Juvenile literature. I. Title.
II. Title: San Francisco Forty-niners.
  GV956.S3L47 2011
  796.332'640979461—dc22
                        2010017461

TABLE OF CONTENTS

Chapter 1 ....Continued Greatness, 4

Chapter 2 ....The Beginning of the 49ers, 10

Chapter 3 ....The NFL Era Begins, 16

Chapter 4 ....A New Era, 22

Chapter 5 ....The Glory Years, 28

Chapter 6 ....Passing the Torch, 34

Timeline, 42

Quick Stats, 44

Quotes and Anecdotes, 45

Glossary, 46

For More Information, 47

Index, 48

About the Author, 48

CONTINUED GREATNESS

The 75,129 fans at Joe Robbie Stadium in Miami, Florida, could sense what was about to happen. With 3:20 left, the Cincinnati Bengals led the San Francisco 49ers 16–13 in Super Bowl XXIII. The 49ers had the ball, but on their own eight-yard line. They would need a field goal to tie or a touchdown to win. The Bengals just had to stop them. That was easier said than done.

San Francisco had come into Super Bowl XXIII with a dynamic offense. Quarterback Joe Montana was considered one of the best in the National Football League (NFL). Running back Roger Craig had a career-high 2,036 total yards of offense that season. Future Hall of Fame wide receiver Jerry Rice was just coming into his prime. But throughout the game, the Bengals defense held the 49ers mostly in check.

Both defenses were strong in the first half. The teams went into halftime tied 3–3.

49ERS QUARTERBACK JOE MONTANA DROPS BACK TO SEARCH FOR AN OPEN RECEIVER DURING SUPER BOWL XXIII.

Both teams added a field goal in the third quarter to stay even at 6–6. But then Cincinnati's Stanford Jennings returned a kickoff for 93 yards and a touchdown to close out the third quarter.

That woke up the 49ers offense. Montana drove the team 85 yards in four plays. He finished the drive with a 14-yard touchdown pass to Rice. But Cincinnati would soon answer when kicker Jim Breech made his third field goal of the day.

With the Bengals leading 16–13, Montana led the 49ers offense back on the field.

WELCOME TO THE HALL OF FAME

Many credit coach Bill Walsh for San Francisco's dominance during the 1980s. But he certainly had a lot of talented players to work with, too. The talent included four future Hall of Fame players. They were Joe Montana, Jerry Rice, Ronnie Lott, and Fred Dean. To his credit, Walsh is also in the Hall of Fame.

Without the slightest sign of nerves, Montana began the drive. One play after another, he moved down the field. Montana connected with his top receiver, Rice, three times. The last of these was a 27-yard strike to put the 49ers in the red zone.

The Bengals figured Montana would try to go to Rice again, this time in the end zone. But the quarterback had other plans. Montana found John Taylor for a 10-yard touchdown pass that capped off an 11-play, 92-yard drive. San Francisco had won 20–16.

It is hard to believe that the 49ers were ever losing the game. San Francisco had 453 offensive yards that day to Cincinnati's 229. Rice set a Super Bowl record with 215 receiving yards while catching 11 passes. Montana completed 23 of his 36 passes for a record 357 yards.

JERRY RICE MAKES A FINGERTIP CATCH DURING SUPER BOWL XXIII.

The 49ers were a dominant team during the 1980s. That thrilling drive in January 1989 secured the team's third Super Bowl victory. The first two had also come during that decade. A fourth Super Bowl victory would also be won after the 1989 season.

The 49ers showed their renowned passing attack in Super Bowl XXIII. Coach Bill

ROGER CRAIG

Roger Craig was one of the 49ers' top running backs during their era of greatness in the 1980s. He was known for his high-knee running technique. During the 1985 season, he became the first NFL player to rush for 1,000 yards while also tallying 1,000 receiving yards during the same season. Craig also became the first player to score three touchdowns in a Super Bowl, a feat he did in Super Bowl XIX against the Miami Dolphins. He was named the NFL Offensive Player of the Year in 1988.

8   SAN FRANCISCO 49ERS

Walsh was the offensive mastermind. He had a cast of future Hall of Fame players to run his system. Defenses feared the 49ers. If Montana was not passing to one of his star receivers—Rice, Taylor, or Dwight Clark—he was handing the ball off to the versatile running back Craig.

Although the team was known for its offense, the 49ers had a strong defense, too. Anchored by defensive backs Ronnie Lott and Eric Wright, the defense made sure its presence was also felt.

The glory years of the 1980s showed just how high the 49ers had risen since the team's humble beginning in the late 1940s.

JOE MONTANA, JOHN TAYLOR, AND RANDY CROSS CELEBRATE THE GAME-WINNING TOUCHDOWN IN SUPER BOWL XXIII.

JOE COOL AND JERRY RICE

Joe Montana had a reputation for being cool under pressure. Jerry Rice is widely regarded as the greatest receiver to ever play the game. Together they helped the San Francisco 49ers offense strike fear in opposing defenses for years.

During Montana's career, he led his teams to 31 fourth-quarter comebacks. He also threw for more than 40,000 yards and 273 touchdowns during his career. Montana was named the MVP of three Super Bowls and played in eight Pro Bowls.

Rice came out of Mississippi Valley State, a Division I-AA school. He made an immediate impact as a pro. He earned NFC Offensive Rookie of the Year honors in 1985. After his performance in Super Bowl XXIII, Rice became only the third receiver to earn Most Valuable Player honors in the championship game. Montana entered the Pro Football Hall of Fame in 2000. Rice was inducted in 2010.

CHAPTER 2

THE BEGINNING OF THE 49ERS

Anthony J. "Tony" Morabito had a vision. He wanted to bring football to northern California. He had seen the success of college programs in the Bay Area, at Stanford University and the University of California, Berkeley. He believed that a pro football team could also thrive on the West Coast. At the time, there were no major pro sports teams in the San Francisco area.

Morabito tried unsuccessfully to acquire an NFL franchise between 1941 and 1946. He also pursued other options. In 1944, he met with Arch Ward, the sports editor at the *Chicago Tribune*. Ward was working to form a rival football league to the NFL. It was called the All-America Football Conference (AAFC). After failed attempts to join the NFL, Morabito decided to pursue a team in the AAFC. The lumber executive

QUARTERBACK FRANKIE ALBERT, *LEFT*, WAS ONE OF *SPORT MAGAZINE*'S "TOP PERFORMERS" IN 1949.

put down $25,000 to create the San Francisco 49ers. The team would become a charter member of the AAFC. Morabito's dream of owning a pro football franchise had finally come true.

ALL-AMERICA FOOTBALL CONFERENCE

The AAFC began play with eight teams in 1946. The New York Yankees, Brooklyn Dodgers, Buffalo Bisons, and Miami Seahawks made up the Eastern Division. The Cleveland Browns, Chicago Rockets, Los Angeles Dons, and San Francisco 49ers played in the Western Division. The Browns were the only team to win the AAFC championship.

The team made its debut two years later, on August 31, 1946. The 49ers were named in honor of the miners who rushed west in search of gold in 1849. The team's owners came up with the 49ers logo when they saw a photo on the side of a railway freight train. It showed a miner firing a pistol.

The players wore simple uniforms. They had red jerseys with white numbers on the front and back. The pants were white, too. At the time, players wore leather helmets. Approximately 40,000 fans showed up for the 49ers' first home game at Kezar Stadium. It was a preseason game against the Chicago Rockets. The 49ers won the game 34–14. They were ready to make a name for themselves in the AAFC.

On September 8, the 49ers made their regular-season debut against the New York Yankees at Kezar Stadium. It did not go as well as the preseason game. The Yankees rocked the 49ers 21–7. Still, one moment in the game offered a sliver of hope for the future. With the score tied at zero, Johnny Strzykalski hauled in a pass from quarterback Frankie Albert. He then threw a lateral to Len Eshmont, who ran

RUNNING BACK JOHN STRZYKALSKI SCORES A TOUCHDOWN AT NEW YORK IN 1951.

40 yards for a touchdown. That showed the 49ers had the ability to make big plays.

San Francisco finished 9–5 that year. They went 8–4–2 during the next season. Their second season was significant for two reasons. The team began wearing its current red and gold uniforms and also signed its first player of Asian descent, Wally Yonamine.

Fans had high hopes for the 1948 season. They believed the 49ers would win an AAFC championship. The team was still unbeaten after 10 games. But then it had to travel hundreds of miles across the country to take on the Cleveland Browns. The Browns were the dominant team in the AAFC—the defending champions. The powerful 49ers' offense was slowed to a crawl in that game. The Browns defeated the 49ers 14–7. It was the only time during the 1948 season that San Francisco was held to single digits in scoring.

The two teams met again a few weeks later. For the first time in their brief history, the 49ers played a game that held a great deal of importance. The 49ers needed to beat the Browns to stay in contention for the league championship. They were up for the challenge but failed to knock off Cleveland. The 49ers fell by a score of 31–28. It was the heartbreaking moment of a 12–2 season.

The 49ers would get a chance for revenge during the next season. After defeating the New York Yankees at Kezar Stadium, the 49ers were to face Cleveland in the championship. A few days before the game, the NFL and AAFC decided to merge into one league. The 49ers-Browns game would be the last game in the AAFC. After that news broke, only 22,550 fans came out to Municipal Stadium in Cleveland, Ohio, for the championship.

THE ESHMONT AWARD

The Eshmont Award is the highest honor a San Francisco 49ers player can earn. The award is given to the player who best displays the type of courageous and inspirational play shown by Len Eshmont.

Eshmont played five seasons with the San Francisco 49ers, including its first season in 1946. He was a running back and defensive back with the team. A former standout at Fordham University, Eshmont rushed for close to 1,200 yards and made 10 interceptions during his career with the 49ers. He died in 1957.

Cleveland scored first, and took a 7–0 lead into halftime. The Browns scored another touchdown in the third quarter to take a 14–0 lead. But the 49ers did not give up. In the fourth

JOHNNY STRZYKALSKI SCORES A TOUCHDOWN AGAINST THE WASHINGTON REDSKINS DURING A 1951 EXHIBITION GAME.

quarter, they drove 74 yards down the field. Albert capped off the drive with a 23-yard touchdown pass to receiver Paul Salata. But that was all the 49ers had. The Browns scored another touchdown and ended up winning 21–7. Despite the muddy conditions, neither team made many mistakes. There were no turnovers and only one penalty in the whole game.

After the 1949 season, the AAFC folded. The San Francisco 49ers played their first NFL season in 1950.

CHAPTER 3

THE NFL ERA BEGINS

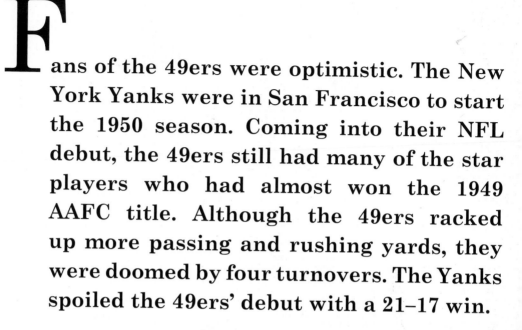

Fans of the 49ers were optimistic. The New York Yanks were in San Francisco to start the 1950 season. Coming into their NFL debut, the 49ers still had many of the star players who had almost won the 1949 AAFC title. Although the 49ers racked up more passing and rushing yards, they were doomed by four turnovers. The Yanks spoiled the 49ers' debut with a 21–17 win.

The 49ers were slow to recover from that first setback. They lost their next four games. Their first season in the NFL ended with a 3–9 record.

The 49ers brought in quarterback Y.A. Tittle in 1951. The team had four winning seasons as he gradually replaced starter Frankie Albert. Another player, Joe Perry, became the kind of tough running back that defined the early years of the NFL. Perry had back-to-back 1,000-yard seasons in 1953 and 1954. He was

R. C. OWENS DEMONSTRATES HIS FAMOUS ALLEY-OOP CATCH DURING A 1957 PRACTICE. HE PLAYED FIVE SEASONS IN SAN FRANCISCO.

the first running back in NFL history to accomplish that feat.

The first two years were filled with injury and disappointment. The 49ers had their best season of their first decade in 1957. The 49ers opened the season with a 20–10 loss to the Chicago Cardinals, but they won their next four games. That led to a showdown with the Chicago Bears on October 27. San Francisco fell behind 17–7. At that point, Morabito suffered a heart attack. He had been sitting in his 50-yard line seat in the lower press box of Kezar Stadium.

Morabito was sometimes a fanatic about his team. He once chased Los Angeles Rams co-owner Fred Levy around the Los Angeles Coliseum locker room looking for a fight. He thought the Rams were playing dirty football. On the day of his heart attack, he did not live long enough to see his 49ers rally back. Late in the game, Tittle threw an 11-yard touchdown pass to Billy Wilson. The heartbroken 49ers dedicated the 21–17 win to Morabito.

The 49ers played another thriller against the Detroit Lions a week later. Tittle threw a 41-yard pass in the fourth quarter. R. C. Owens leaped up over two defenders to make the catch in the end zone. The 49ers

JOE PERRY

The 49ers discovered Joe Perry while he was playing football at a service station during his time in the military. Perry was nicknamed "The Jet." He was the first player in the NFL to gain 1,000 yards in back-to-back seasons. He played in three Pro Bowls and rushed for more than 9,000 yards during his career. He is in the Pro Football Hall of Fame.

JOE "THE JET" PERRY BLASTS THROUGH THE LINE ON HIS WAY TO A TOUCHDOWN IN A 1953 WIN OVER THE GREEN BAY PACKERS.

escaped with a 35–31 victory. The play was known as the alley-oop play and was used often by Tittle and Owens.

Later that season, Tittle had the 49ers on the brink of reaching the championship game. He threw three passes for touchdowns as San Francisco took a 27–7 lead over the Lions. But the Lions roared back and crushed the 49ers' championship dream. They ended up winning 31–27.

The 49ers never won more than seven games for the rest of the decade. Albert had come back as head coach in 1956. After three mediocre seasons, he resigned and was replaced by Red Hickey. Hickey guided the 49ers to back-to-back 7–5 records at the end of the 1950s.

JOE PERRY, *RIGHT*, SHOWS Y. A. TITTLE THE PLASTIC FACE MASK HE WORE IN 1953.

Y. A. AND R. C.

Y. A. Tittle and R. C. Owens provided plenty of highlights for 49ers fans in the 1950s. Tittle was the 1948 rookie of the year with the Baltimore Colts in the AAFC. He joined the 49ers in 1951, after the Colts disbanded. During 10 seasons in San Francisco, he completed 2,427 passes and threw for 33,070 yards. He joined the New York Giants in 1961 and finished his career there. Tittle was the NFL MVP in 1961 and 1963 and also played in seven Pro Bowls.

Owens joined the 49ers in 1957 and stayed there for the next five seasons. He is remembered in San Francisco as one of the most exciting players in team history. During his time there, he racked up 2,926 yards and 20 touchdown catches. Tittle and Owens were most famous for their alley-oop pass in which Owens would jump over defenders to catch the ball. The play became a staple of the 49ers' offense during that era.

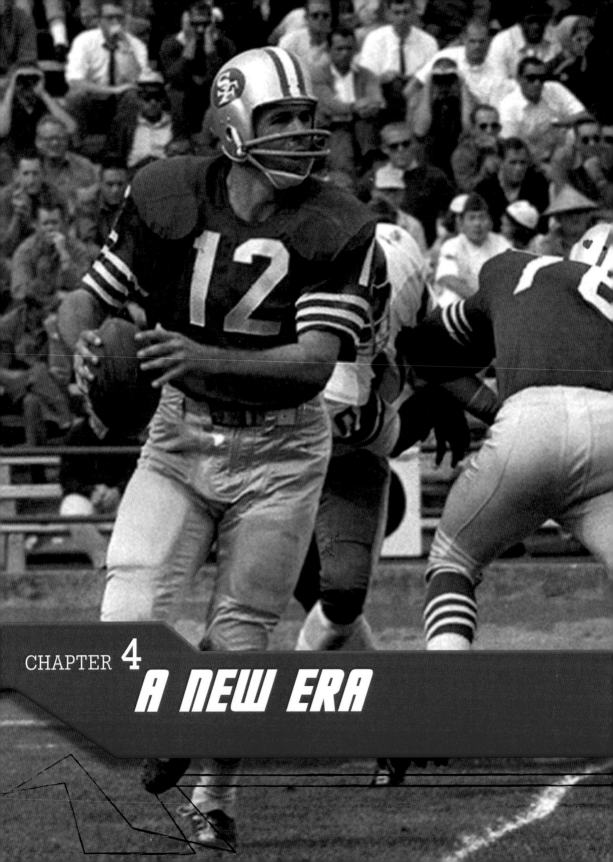

CHAPTER 4

A NEW ERA

Red Hickey played five seasons in the NFL as a tight end. However, his most important contribution to football came as a coach. Hickey took over the 49ers at a time when the fans were becoming frustrated. Their team always seemed to have a shot at the championship only to fall short late in the season.

In 1960, the 49ers started the season 4–4. A game against the mighty Baltimore Colts was on the horizon. The 49ers had a surprise in store for the Colts.

Normally, the quarterback receives the snap while standing just behind the center. Against Baltimore, Hickey decided to have his quarterback stand five yards behind the center at the start of the play. The offensive formation gave the 49ers an extra second or two to develop a play. Hickey also believed it would give the 49ers a chance to knock off the Colts in Baltimore.

The formation was called the shotgun, and the plan worked.

SAN FRANCISCO QUARTERBACK JOHN BRODIE LOOKS FOR A RECEIVER IN A 1963 GAME AGAINST THE MINNESOTA VIKINGS.

The 49ers exploded for more than 200 passing yards behind the play of quarterback John Brodie. But legendary Colts quarterback Johnny Unitas also had a stellar game. He passed for 356 yards. It did not help that Brodie had to be taken out of the game with an injury. Toward the end, the 49ers rookie quarterback Bob Waters led the team down the field for a touchdown drive. The 49ers held on to earn a stunning 30–22 victory.

Defenses, however, soon adjusted to the shotgun offense. Hickey abandoned it in favor of the old T-Formation. The shotgun was not used again until 1975, when the Dallas Cowboys tried it. Today it is a popular formation in both professional and college football.

The 49ers also dealt with a wave of injuries during the 1960s. They did not win more than seven games in any one season during the decade.

Brodie bounced back from injuries in 1965. He threw for more than 3,000 yards in 1965 and connected on 30 touchdown passes. Coach Dick Nolan took over in 1968. The 49ers became a top offensive team that season, but they still finished with a 7–6–1 record.

The 49ers' fortunes changed in 1970. They won their first National Football Conference (NFC) West Division title. They

DICK NOLAN

Dick Nolan was the coach of the 49ers from 1968 until 1975. He had a regular season record of 54–53–5. Nolan guided the team to three playoff appearances, but his final three years were miserable. San Francisco finished with a losing record each time. The struggles ignited almost violent backlash from the fans, forcing Nolan out of a job. Nolan is known as one of the creators of the flex defense. He passed away in 2007.

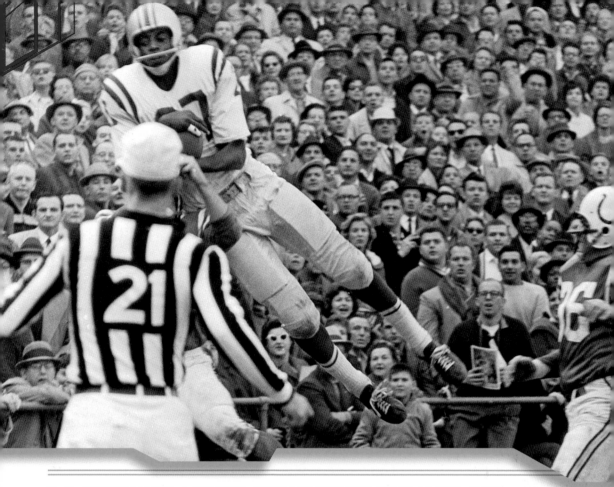

R. C. OWENS MAKES A LEAPING CATCH IN THE END ZONE AS THE 49ERS UPSET THE COLTS IN 1960.

also won their first playoff game, a 17–14 victory on the road against the Minnesota Vikings. Brodie was the league's Most Valuable Player (MVP). He threw for more than 2,900 yards and 24 touchdowns. 49ers cornerback Bruce Taylor was named the defensive rookie of the year.

The 49ers moved into Candlestick Park in 1971. Many key players returned from the 10–3–1 team from the season before. But the 49ers lost two of their first four games. One was at home to the rival Los Angeles Rams.

San Francisco would lose only three more games during the regular season. They marched into the playoffs and beat the Washington Redskins in the first round. The 49ers then renewed their rivalry with the Dallas Cowboys. Dallas had knocked San Francisco out of the playoffs the year before. The 49ers fell short again. Turnovers doomed the 49ers in a 14–3 loss.

The 49ers would get another postseason shot at the Cowboys in 1972. The team had started slow, and Brodie suffered an injury. Steve Spurrier stepped in as quarterback and played spectacular football. He guided the 49ers to a 6–2 record over their final eight games. San Francisco earned its third straight division title. They opened the playoffs against the Cowboys at Candlestick Park. The 49ers were ahead 28–13 in the fourth quarter. But the Cowboys rallied to crush the championship dream of the 49ers with a 30–28 win.

The 49ers would not play in another postseason game for nine years. However, the foundation for the glory years of the 1980s was also being laid.

CANDLESTICK PARK

The San Francisco Giants began playing baseball in Candlestick Park in 1960. It was originally named Bay View Stadium, but was changed to Candlestick after a name-the-park contest in 1959. The stadium was known for its swirling winds, despite the fact that it had been designed to prevent the wind from having an impact on the game.

LINEBACKER DAVE WILCOX WAS INDUCTED INTO THE PRO FOOTBALL HALL OF FAME IN 2000. HE ANCHORED THE 49ERS DEFENSE FOR 11 SEASONS.

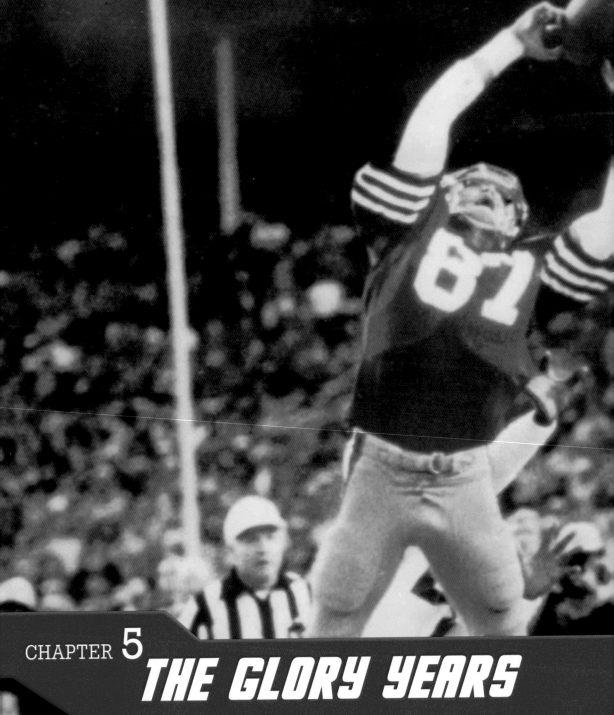

CHAPTER 5
THE GLORY YEARS

Ohio businessman Ed DeBartolo Jr. bought the 49ers before the start of the 1977 season. His early years as the team owner were miserable. The 49ers failed to win more than five games during those first three seasons. The team hit a low in 1978 when it finished 2–14.

The 49ers finished 2–14 in 1979 as well, but there was a different feel to everything taking place. The team had hired Bill Walsh as its new head coach, and he began installing his signature West Coast Offense. The 49ers had also drafted a quarterback from Notre Dame in 1979. His name was Joe Montana.

Montana earned the starting job by the end of the 1980 season. In 1981, he led the 49ers to a 13–3 record and NFC West Division title. The 49ers held off the New York Giants 38–24 in the first round of the playoffs. Then they hosted the Dallas Cowboys in the NFC Championship Game. That game would

DWIGHT CLARK LEAPS TO CATCH JOE MONTANA'S PASS IN THE FOURTH QUARTER OF THE 1982 NFC CHAMPIONSHIP GAME. THE TOUCHDOWN AND EXTRA POINT GAVE THE 49ERS A 28–27 WIN OVER THE DALLAS COWBOYS.

"THE GENIUS"

Bill Walsh had to wait until he was 47 to become an NFL head coach. Even then, he spent only 10 seasons in that position, all with the 49ers. He made the most of his time. Walsh inherited a poorly managed, losing team. Within just three years, the 49ers were Super Bowl champions and beginning a streak of dominance in the NFL. During that time, he became nicknamed "The Genius" for his schemes that became known as the West Coast Offense.

Walsh lead the 49ers to three Super Bowl titles and six division titles. He was named the league's best coach in 1981 and 1984 and won 102 games during his career. Walsh retired from NFL coaching in 1988, before the 49ers fourth Super Bowl, because he was burned out from coaching. He entered the Hall of Fame in 1993. After a three-year struggle with leukemia, Walsh died in 2007. He was 75.

become one of the most memorable games in NFL history.

San Francisco trailed the Cowboys by six points with 51 seconds remaining. Montana took the snap inside the Cowboys' 10-yard line. He ran to his right to avoid the rush. Then Montana launched a pass to the back corner of the end zone. There, wide receiver Dwight Clark seemingly came out of nowhere to make a leaping catch in front of Dallas' Everson Walls. The play became known as "The Catch." With a 28–27 victory, the 49ers finally broke through to the Super Bowl.

At Super Bowl XVI, the 49ers defeated the Cincinnati Bengals 26–21. Montana was named the MVP. But the defense made a key stop to preserve the win. When the Bengals had a first down on the goal line, the 49ers defense

THE PLAYERS CARRIED COACH BILL WALSH OFF THE FIELD AFTER SAN FRANCISCO BEAT THE MIAMI DOLPHINS IN SUPER BOWL XIX.

held them out of the end zone four times.

Super Bowl XVI was the start of a special era for the 49ers. They were adored by their fans and feared by opponents throughout the 1980s. The 49ers won eight division titles in a 10-year period from 1981–1990. They made the playoffs nine times during that span and won all four Super Bowls in which they appeared.

The 49ers reached the NFC Championship Game again in 1983 but lost to the Washington Redskins. Two controversial calls helped lead to the result. The 49ers came into the 1984 season determined to make up for that loss. They dominated opponents on their way to a 15–1 regular season. Their only loss was to the Pittsburgh Steelers. In the playoffs, the 49ers rolled past the New York Giants and then the Chicago Bears. Their defense, led by Ronnie Lott and Fred Dean, made nine sacks against the Bears.

Up next was a date with the high-scoring Miami Dolphins in Super Bowl XIX. Montana was upset about all the coverage Miami quarterback Dan Marino was receiving. The 49ers quarterback used it as motivation. He led the 49ers to a 38–16 win.

The 49ers defeated the Cincinnati Bengals again to win Super Bowl XXIII in 1989. Their decade of dominance ended with another Super Bowl in 1990. The 49ers went 14–2 during that regular season. After dominating the Minnesota Vikings and Los Angeles Rams in the playoffs, the 49ers faced quarterback John Elway and the Denver Broncos in Super Bowl XXIV.

San Francisco dominated all aspects of the game in a 55–10 victory. The win secured the 49ers' legacy as the team of the 1980s. After the 49ers' fourth Super Bowl, some considered them to be one of the greatest NFL franchises of all time.

JERRY RICE AND THE 49ERS BEAT THE BRONCOS IN SUPER BOWL XXIV.

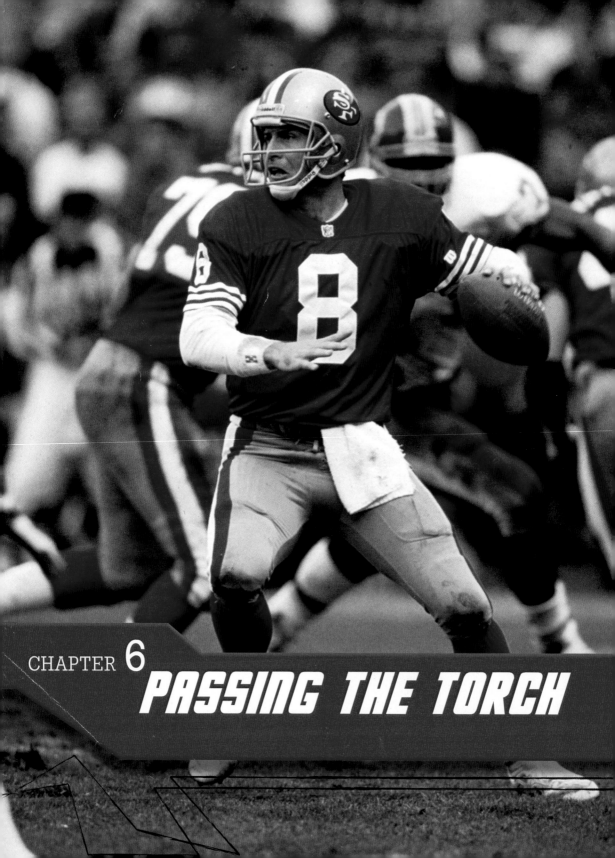

CHAPTER 6

PASSING THE TORCH

The San Francisco 49ers entered the 1990 season as the two-time defending Super Bowl champions. Having already won a Super Bowl under new coach George Seifert, and with the roster still intact, the players were confident they could win a third straight.

The team looked like they could do it during the regular season. Joe Montana led the 49ers to a 14–2 record, but the journey would be cut short in the playoffs. The 49ers faced the New York Giants in the NFC Championship Game. With San Francisco leading by four in the fourth quarter, Giants defensive lineman Leonard Marshall hit Montana hard. The quarterback suffered a serious injury. He also fumbled the ball. After the Giants recovered it, they marched down the field for a field goal. The 49ers' lead was cut to 13–12. The Giants would get one more field goal to win the game and head to the Super Bowl.

QUARTERBACK STEVE YOUNG DID HIS BEST TO PICK UP WHERE JOE MONTANA LEFT OFF IN SAN FRANCISCO.

Montana was out for the entire 1991 season. That opened the door for Steve Young. The new quarterback quickly became a star with the best passer rating that season. But Young missed five games with a knee injury, and the 49ers missed the playoffs for the first time in eight seasons.

STEVE YOUNG

The Tampa Bay Buccaneers traded Steve Young to San Francisco in 1987. Young went on to become one of only two quarterbacks in NFL history to win six passing titles. The Hall of Fame quarterback threw for 33,124 yards and 232 touchdowns. He also rushed for 43 touchdowns and was named the league MVP twice.

Young was the MVP of the league in 1992. He led San Francisco to a 14–2 record in the regular season. There was a brief quarterback controversy before the team's final game. Montana replaced Young as the starter for that game. It was Montana's first game since 1990. Young returned to the starting role for the 49ers' playoff game against the Washington Redskins the next week. The 49ers beat the Redskins 20–13. But they lost to the eventual Super Bowl champion Dallas Cowboys 30–20 in the next game.

Young's play in 1993 made 49ers fans start to think about the future instead of the past. The new quarterback passed for more than 4,000 yards that season and led the team to a 10–6 record. But after beating the New York Giants in the playoffs, the 49ers lost a close game to the Dallas Cowboys in the NFC Championship Game.

DEION SANDERS MADE HIS ONLY SEASON IN SAN FRANCISCO A MEMORABLE ONE. HE IS CONSIDERED ONE OF THE TOP CORNERBACKS IN NFL HISTORY.

SOME 49ERS PLAYERS DOUSE COACH GEORGE SEIFERT NEAR THE END OF
SUPER BOWL XXIX. THE 49ERS BEAT SAN DIEGO 49–26.

With a core of good players, the 49ers added two more super-stars for the next season. They were defensive back Deion Sand-ers and linebacker Ken Norton Jr. With the new players, San Francisco had pushed itself to the next level. Despite a sluggish 3–2 start, the 49ers then won 10 straight games. With a 13–3 record, they won the division.

The 49ers defeated the Bears in the first round of the

playoffs. That set up another battle with the Cowboys. Out for revenge, the 49ers scored 21 points in the first five minutes of the game. They dazzled the Candlestick Park crowd with a 38–28 win over the defending Super Bowl champions.

Young had finally guided the 49ers to a Super Bowl. Now they were heavy favorites against the San Diego Chargers. The 49ers lived up to the billing. Young threw a 44-yard pass to Jerry Rice early in Super Bowl XXIX, and the 49ers never let go of the momentum. The 49ers defeated the Chargers 49–26. Young threw six touchdown passes in the win. The 49ers became the first team to win five Super Bowls.

The 49ers continued to be a contender after the 1994 season. With Young as quarterback, they made the playoffs in each of the next four seasons. The team even made the NFC Championship Game in 1997. But soon San Francisco began to struggle.

T.O.

The 49ers selected talented but controversial wide receiver Terrell Owens in the 1996 NFL Draft. Owens played eight seasons with the 49ers. He racked up more than 8,000 yards and 81 touchdowns during that span. But his time in San Francisco did not end well. He had trouble getting along with teammates. In 2003, Owens and the 49ers split on bad terms. Owens would later go on to be a star receiver for the Philadelphia Eagles, Dallas Cowboys, and Buffalo Bills. But controversy seemed to follow him wherever he went.

In 1999, Young suffered a career-ending injury. The team lost 11 of its 13 remaining games after Young's injury. The 49ers' string of 16 straight 10-win seasons came to a halt as they finished 4–12. It was their first losing record since 1982.

VERNON DAVIS SEARCHES FOR OPEN FIELD AGAINST THE TENNESSEE TITANS IN 2009. THE 49ERS DRAFTED HIM SIXTH OVERALL IN 2006.

San Francisco recovered a bit, making playoff appearances in 2001 and 2002. But the 49ers have never regained the success of the 1980s and early 1990s. The team went 7–9 in 2003 and 2–14 in 2004—the worst record in the NFL. Dick Nolan's son, Mike Nolan, was named 49ers coach in 2005. With the number

A FUTURE STAR?

In 2006, the 49ers drafted tight end Vernon Davis with the sixth overall pick. With great size, speed, and strength, some considered him to be one of the top tight ends in the NFL before he even played a game. He has lived up to the hype. In four seasons with the 49ers, Davis has already racked up 2,097 yards and has caught 22 touchdown passes. He also helped his team finish with an 8–8 record in 2009. That ended a six-year streak of losing seasons for the 49ers.

one draft pick that year, the 49ers took quarterback Alex Smith from Utah. But it made little difference. The 49ers continued to struggle.

The team has since added talented players through the draft. Tight end Vernon Davis, the team's 2006 first-round pick, is trying to add his name to the long list of 49ers receiving greats. Linebacker Patrick Willis immediately established himself as one of the top defensive players in the league after being taken in the first round of the 2007 draft.

The 49ers saw a glimmer of hope for the future in 2009. Under coach Mike Singletary, the team finished 8–8, the team's first non-losing record since 2002. However, the 49ers still had a long way to go to match the heights of their glory years in the 1980s.

A "BEAST"

The 49ers drafted a bright young star on offense in 2006 when they added tight end Vernon Davis. In the 2007 NFL Draft, they added a bright young star on defense, too. The 49ers drafted middle linebacker Patrick Willis eleventh overall. The man whom one scout called a "beast" was named Defensive Rookie of the Year. He had an NFL-best 174 tackles during that rookie season.

Willis has established himself as a force on defense. In his first three seasons, he had 358 career tackles, nine sacks, and four interceptions. He made the Pro Bowl in each of his first three seasons and is considered one of the top players in the game at his position.

TIMELINE

1944	A meeting is held on June 4 to discuss the formation of the AAFC. The 49ers become charter members of the league.
1946	The 49ers make their regular-season debut against the New York Yankees at Kezar Stadium on September 8. San Francisco loses the game 21–7.
1949	In a game in which the winner would advance to the AAFC Championship Game, the 49ers knock off the Yankees 17–7 December 4 at Kezar Stadium.
1949	The 49ers take on the Cleveland Browns in the championship game December 11 at Municipal Stadium in Cleveland. The 49ers lose 21–7.
1950	The 49ers make their NFL debut on September 17 in a 21–17 loss to the New York Yanks at Kezar Stadium.
1950	After dropping its first five games, San Francisco wins its first NFL game on October 22, defeating the Detroit Lions 28–27.
1957	Team owner Anthony J. "Tony" Morabito dies of a heart attack while watching the 49ers take on the Chicago Bears October 27 at Kezar Stadium.
1960	Coach Red Hickey uses the shotgun formation for the first time against the Baltimore Colts on November 27.
1972	San Francisco plays its final game at Kezar Stadium on January 3, falling 17–10 to the Dallas Cowboys in the NFC Championship Game.

1982 Dwight Clark makes "The Catch" in the end zone as the 49ers stun the Dallas Cowboys 28–27 and advance to their first Super Bowl on January 10.

1982 San Francisco defeats the Cincinnati Bengals 26–21 in Super Bowl XVI on January 24.

1985 Against the media-favorite Miami Dolphins, the 49ers overcome a 10–7 score to win 38–16 in Super Bowl XIX on January 20.

1989 Facing the Bengals for the second time in a Super Bowl, the 49ers rally with a 92-yard scoring drive to win 20–16 in Super Bowl XXIII on January 22.

1990 Against the rival Los Angeles Rams, the 49ers dominate the NFC Championship Game and march back to the Super Bowl with a 30–3 victory on January 14.

1990 San Francisco defeats the Denver Broncos 55–10 in Super Bowl XXIV on January 28.

1995 San Francisco defeats the Dallas Cowboys 38–28 in the NFC Championship Game on January 15.

1995 The 49ers win a record fifth Super Bowl with a convincing 49–26 win over the San Diego Chargers in Super Bowl XXIX on January 29.

2009 The 49ers finish 8–8 for the team's first non-losing season since 2002.

QUICK STATS

FRANCHISE HISTORY

1946–1949 (AAFC)
1950– (NFL)

SUPER BOWLS
(wins in bold)

1981 (XVI), 1984 (XIX), 1988 (XXIII), 1989 (XXIV), 1994 (XXIX)

AAFC CHAMPIONSHIP GAMES
(1946–49)

1949

NFC CHAMPIONSHIP GAMES
(since 1970 AFL-NFL merger)

1970, 1971, 1981, 1983, 1984, 1988, 1989, 1990, 1992, 1993, 1994, 1997

KEY PLAYERS
(position, seasons with team)

Dwight Clark (WR, 1979–87)
Roger Craig (RB/FB, 1983–90)
Vernon Davis (TE, 2006–)
Fred Dean (DE, 1981–85)
Ronnie Lott (DB 1981–90)
Joe Montana (QB, 1979–92)
Joe Perry (RB, 1948–60, 1963)
Jerry Rice (WR 1985–2000)
Y. A. Tittle (QB, 1951–60)
Dave Wilcox (LB, 1964–74)
Patrick Willis (LB, 2007–)
Steve Young (QB, 1987–99)

KEY COACHES

George Seifert (1989–96): 98–30;
    10–5 (playoffs)
Bill Walsh (1979–88): 92–59–1;
    10–4 (playoffs)

HOME FIELDS

Candlestick Park (1971–)
    The stadium has been known by
    other names during this time.
Kezar Stadium (1946–70)

* All statistics through 2009 season

QUOTES AND ANECDOTES

The NFL became violent in nature in the 1950s. Several 49ers capitalized on the vicious style of football. In 1953, Cleveland Browns quarterback Otto Graham had his jaw slashed open when he took an elbow to the face by an unidentified member of the 49ers.

Jerry Rice's spectacular speed helped him become a star football player in high school. The discovery of Rice's talent came about in an unusual way. The school principal once tracked Rice down, and when he called his name, Rice ran off. The principal called him into the office the next morning and gave him five or six lashings with a thick strap. Later, though, the man told the football coach about Rice's speed.

"Well, I'm an old country boy, and I used to go hunting with a shotgun," Red Hickey said when describing the shotgun offense. "How about we call it the shotgun?"

"This is just a tremendous loss for all of us, especially to the Bay Area because of what he meant to the 49ers," Joe Montana said after the death of Bill Walsh. "Outside of my dad he was probably the most influential person in my life. I am going to miss him."

In a *Monday Night Football* game in Seattle in October 2002, then-49ers wide receiver Terrell Owens pulled a permanent marker out of his sock after catching a touchdown pass. He then proceeded to autograph the ball and hand it to his financial adviser. The adviser was sitting in an end zone luxury suite rented by Shawn Springs, the cornerback Owens had just beaten on the play.

GLOSSARY

flex defense

A defensive system in which the defensive linemen line up in different areas based on what the other team's offense might try.

49er

Someone who took part in the California gold rush of 1849.

hall of fame

A place built to honor noteworthy achievements by athletes in their respective sports.

Heisman Trophy

An award given to the top college football player each year.

legacy

Anything handed down from the past.

media

Various forms of communication, including television, radio, and newspapers; the press or news reporting agencies.

merge

To unite into a single body.

momentum

Associated with periods of competition, such as a win streak, in which everything seems to go right for the competitors.

red zone

The area on a football field between the end zone and the 20-yard line.

shotgun formation

An offensive formation in which the quarterback lines up three or four yards behind the center to allow him more time to pass.

T-Formation

An offensive formation in which two running backs line up behind or on either side of the quarterback.

West Coast Offense

An offense that uses a variety of formations to confuse a defense. It uses a short passing game designed to control the football.

Further Reading

Harris, David. *The Genius: How Bill Walsh Reinvented Football and Created an NFL Dynasty*. New York, NY: Random House, 2008.

Myers, Gary, and Joe Montana. *The Catch: One Play, Two Dynasties, and the Game That Changed the NFL*. New York, NY: Random House, 2009.

Rice, Jerry. *Go Long! My Journey Beyond the Game and the Fame*. New York, NY: Ballantine Books, 2007.

Web Links

To learn more about the San Francisco 49ers, visit ABDO Publishing Company online at **www.abdopublishing.com**. Web sites about the 49ers are featured on our Book Links page. These links are routinely monitored and updated to provide the most current information available.

Places to Visit

Candlestick Park
602 Jamestown Ave.
San Francisco, California 94124
408-562-4949
www.49ers.com/stadium/stadium-info.html
This is the home field for the 49ers. The 49ers play eight regular-season home games every year.

Pro Football Hall of Fame
2121 George Halas Dr., NW
Canton, OH 44708
330-456-8207
www.profootballhof.com
This hall of fame and museum highlights the greatest players and moments in the history of the National Football League. Eighteen people affiliated with the 49ers are enshrined, including Joe Montana, Jerry Rice, and Y. A. Tittle.

San Francisco 49ers Office
4949 Centennial Blvd.
Santa Clara, CA 95054
408-562-4949
www.sf49ers.com
The team's headquarters and practice facilities are here.

INDEX

Albert, Frankie, 12, 15, 17, 21
All-America Football
    Conference, 11–15, 17, 21

Baltimore Colts, 21, 23
Brodie, John, 24, 25, 26
Brooklyn Dodgers, 12
Buffalo Bills, 39
Buffalo Bisons, 12

Candlestick Park (Bay View
    Stadium), 25, 26, 39
Chicago Bears, 18, 32, 38
Chicago Cardinals, 18,
Chicago Rockets, 12
Cincinnati Bengals, 5–6,
    30–31, 32
Clark, Dwight, 9, 30
Cleveland Browns, 12, 13–15
Craig, Roger, 5, 7, 9

Dallas Cowboys, 26, 29–30,
    36, 39
Davis, Vernon, 40, 41
Dean, Fred, 6, 32
DeBartolo Jr., Ed (owner), 29
Denver Broncos, 32
Detroit Lions, 17, 18

Eshmont, Len, 12–13, 14

Hickey, Red (coach), 21, 23

Kezar Stadium, 12, 14, 18

Los Angeles Dons, 12
Los Angeles Raiders, 32
Los Angeles Rams, 18, 25, 32
Lott, Ronnie, 6, 9, 32

Miami Dolphins, 7, 32
Miami Seahawks, 12
Minnesota Vikings, 25, 32
Montana, Joe, 5–6, 9, 29, 30,
    32, 35, 36
Morabito, Anthony J. "Tony"
    (owner), 11–12, 18

New York Giants, 29, 32, 35,
    36
New York Jets, 32
New York Yankees, 12, 14
New York Yanks, 17
Nolan, Dick (coach), 24, 40
Nolan, Mike (coach), 40
Norton Jr., Ken, 38

Owens, R. C., 21
Owens, Terrell, 39

Perry, Joe, 18
Philadelphia Eagles, 39
Pittsburgh Steelers, 32

Rice, Jerry, 5–6, 9, 39, 41

Salata, Paul, 15
San Diego Chargers, 39
Sanders, Deion, 38
Seifert, George (coach), 35
shotgun formation, 23–24
Singletary, Mike (coach), 41
Smith, Alex, 41
Spurrier, Steve, 26
Strzykalski, Johnny, 12
Super Bowl XVI, 30–31
Super Bowl XIX, 7, 32
Super Bowl XXIII, 5–6, 7, 9, 32
Super Bowl XXIV, 7, 32
Super Bowl XXIX, 39

Tampa Bay Buccaneers, 36
Taylor, Bruce, 25
Taylor, John, 6,
Tittle, Y. A., 17, 18, 21

Walsh, Bill (coach), 6, 7–8, 29,
    30
Washington Redskins, 26, 31,
    36
Waters, Bob, 24
West Coast Offense, 29, 30
Willis, Patrick, 41
Wilson, Billy, 18
Wright, Eric, 9

Yonamine, Wally, 13
Young, Steve, 36, 39

About the Author

Brian Lester is a sports writer in Findlay, Ohio, where he lives with his wife and daughter. He has covered athletics at every level, from high school to the pros, and has spent the last eight years covering the University of Findlay for *The Courier* in Findlay. He was named the best sports writer in Virginia in the nondaily newspaper category in 1998 and has won two Associated Press Awards in Ohio.